BREATHING SPACES

William Meroney

BREATHING SPACES

William Meroney, Author

ISBN 978-1-955338-27-1

Printed in the United States of America

Pocahontas Press

Prologue

Whatever value these poems have for others, I have come to realize that much of their value to me lies in their unique ability to reflect the places and times of my life. I like to think that this is not a selfish sentiment, but rather the action of those times and places working their meaning through me. In poetry, as in nothing else (including philosophy), the places and times I have lived in and through show themselves as expressions in the words I have used. Not just the words but their placement, their sound and their cadence. My poetry takes its life from the places where I have been and the times I have been there, sometimes as immediate experience, sometimes as recalled or reimagined experience, and sometimes as my experience of the poetry of others. So, I have ranged over my own times and places but also thousands of years of poetry.

As I see it, poetry lives where speech dies out, where the last word has been said, in the silence that lingers when there seems nothing more can be said, a space without the sound of words. In the depth of this silence a poem forms - words in the mind of a poet, words escaping the limits of their own language, balances in time in their place in the poem.

This book is the fruit of a strange vocation: perhaps this vocation could simply be called 'living', yet to see living as a vocation may seem out of place. After all, we all live. A vocation is something we do, usually something we choose to do. Yet, the words in this book were not chosen so freely, rather they are words that found me as I was living at a particular place and time and were gracious enough to allow me to pick them up and place them on these pages. It is only in looking back over my life that I have come to feel these words as truly my words, in a way that nothing else I have written or said does. If a vocation is where you have been called to put your life's deepest energies, then fashioning the words in this book has been my vocation. I hope they work as poems, yet I do not claim to have led the life of a poet or claim poetry as my vocation. At the end of his great poem, "Estetique du Mal", Wallace Stevens sees the world:

> As if the air, the mid-day air, was swarming
> With the metaphysical changes that occur
> Merely in living as and where we live.

This is the world as I have found it. I can lay some claim to a conventional vocation of a philosopher, and here I hope I have been able to sense a few of these metaphysical changes and bring them to life on these pages.

Dedication

Perhaps the most important time and place animating these pages is one that animates the title, **Breathing Spaces**, arising from my recollection of a conversation with my father. I think of this conversation now, and thought of it then, as a young philosopher talking to a linguist. As a philosopher I want to know if propositions mean something more than marks on a page. My father, ever the linguist but also a poet, sees the words 'sentence' and 'sentience' as cognates, he sees apprehending a sentence as breathing the words on the page, not merely as marks, but as marks together with the spaces between them. The spaces become essential to the apprehension of the words of the sentence and breathing brings their meaning to life.

For helping me see breathing space as essential to meaning in words and life, I dedicate this book to my father.

The many forms of fascination
are lost on the chrysalis
Desire alone moves it on
Past the blocks the mind sets
In the eye that looks toward God
Past the snares of solitude's
Thoughts thinking of themselves

In desire two minds become as one
Creating wings where once were none

CONTENTS

UNCOMMON MEASURES

A Primitive Silence

Evocation *4*
Venetian Lagoon *6*
L'Entre Deux Guerres *7*
Chance Meeting *9*
To the Old Man from Milford *10*
Anasazi *11*
Hanuman *12*
Daybreak at Brownbacks *13*
Dialectic *14*
Serenity *15*
Appearances *16*
Still Life *17*
Opposition *18*
Found Poems *19*
Writer's Block *20*
Constructions in One Dimension *21*
A Whimsical Ontology *22*
Wallace Stevens at the Barbecue *23*
Memoir of a Girl Who Lost Her Life
        Shadowboxing in Griffith Park *24*
Baling Hay in Valley Forge *25*
Along the Wissahicken *26*
During a Lull in the Fighting *27*
Raid on the Inarticulate *28*
Search for a Method *29*
The Desire to Live in the Present *30*
The Quiet Drum *31*
The Sun Sets Every Day *32*
Emerging from the Tunnel *33*
Secondary Properties *34*

The Hangmans' Songs 35

Another Life

    Shorelines *50*

    Spring Light *51*

    The End of Something *52*

    A Second Son. *53*

    Solitary Conversations *56*

    Milford Spring. *57*

    Sunrise at Sligo Creek *59*

    A Long Story. *60*

    Looking for Italian Brandy in the French Quarter *61*

    An Unexpected Sunrise. *62*

    Palm Trees and Possibilities. *63*

    Dayfire *64*

    Olmec Colossal Head. *65*

    The Death of a Minor Morris. *66*

    The Ontology of Lost Moments *67*

    North & South *73*

AGAINST TIME

Light in the East

    Morning. *78*

    Out West. *79*

    The Ocean Has No Name. *80*

    Early Rain, Morning Clouds *81*

    The World as Photograph *82*

    Transcendence in Blue & Green *83*

    Cornfield at Night. *84*

    Autumn Dust *85*

    Late Fall. *86*

    Love's Condensate. *87*

    Controlled Burning *88*

    Above Caesar's Head *89*

Caesar's Head Revisited 90
Barn Work 91
Crosscurrents 93
Transformation 94
Remembrance 95
Art Film 96
The Place of Solitude 97
Lovers' Questions 98
Dream Shadows. 99
Takoma Station. 100
Car Talk 101

Moving West
Via Negativa. 105
Cesar Vallejo: Reflection 106
Turner at Large. 107
Merovingian Memory 108
Phidias at Night 109
Admonition for the New Day. 110
Sappho Out of Time. 112
Scholars at Dinner. 113
The Battle of Salimas. 114
Plato's Ghost 115

RECOLLECTIONS

Stepping Stones
(Poems in Transition)
Alte Musik 121
Terms and Conditions 123
Crossing the Water. 124
Across the Threshold. 125
In Reason's Shadow 126
Night Terror 127
On Purifications 128

Final Sun 129
Measure Zero. 130
Another Look. 131
Touching Down in Denver. 132
Silence of the Lands 134

Ridgelines
(Poems and Afterthoughts)

    Blue Rider. 137
    Laurel Fork Creek 138
    Sun over Plywood 139
    And so the Light Goes. 140
    Leaving Santa Fe. 141
    Marginalia 142
    Shaking Realism 143
    Regretfullness. 144
    Coming Home on Sunday Morning 145
    Sound and Fury. 146
    Cappucinni Convento Amalfi. 147
    Before the Fall 148
    Fragment Outside Time 150
    Revisitation. 151
    Colossus Regained 152
    Against the Grain 153
    Form as Formlessness 154
    Thirty West Wyneva 156
    Our 20th Century. 158
    Moonsight. 159

After Images
(Retentions and Reflections)

    Words for Painting Perhaps. 163
    Dust Down a Country Road. 164
    As I Leave the Room 165
    Redemption. 166

Anachron 167
Silken Weavings 168
Lost Languages 169
Finding the Falconer 170
Time and Again 171
Christmas Below Zero 172

Magic Horses
(Early and Uncollected Poems)

Magic Horses 175
Phaeton 176
I Built a Castle Once 177
Day Dawning 178
Eagles Fly 179
Go Outside 180
The Shade 181
Icy Night of Sirius 183
Foolish Heart 184
Love's a Human Thing 185
Cycles 186
December Summer 187
Dead Tree in Fall 189
Desert Silence 190
To Restore is to Destroy 191
Evening in New Jersey 192

Notes on Poems **195**

Bibliography **197**

UNCOMMON MEASURES

*Poetry is Love's own craft, whereby all forms of life
are begotten and produced.*

Plato
The Symposium

A Primitive Silence

Die Grenzen der Sprache...
Die Grenzen meiner Welt bedueten.

Ludwig Wittgenstein
Tractatus Logico-Philosophicus

Le silence
Est monte de ton livre vers ton coeur.

Yves Bonnefoy
Un feu va devant nous

EVOCATION

I

I speak and set myself
Apart from beast and nature
Define, by artifice of signs
Speech as language, man as symbol

At the center of symbols
Otherwise insignificant except
For silent soundings seen
In speech, song, and laughter.

II

Speech echoes sounds
Of time before birth
Before our birth
Before the birth of time

Time born not of time
But of song outside time
The inner sense
Of dream and desire

The progeny of laughter
Demonic, angelic, endless
Human and unknown.

III

We are born, perhaps
Not in, but into, time
Into the arms of the living
Into the river of dreams.

So come, my child, and share
My life and all it means:
My open arms, my song
My laughter and my dreams.

VENETIAN LAGOON

Seek in me the death

You never found in life

Scattered

Like sea-birds' nests

Across the face

Of the waters.

L'ENTRE DEUX GUERRES

I

How do we dream
The eternal dream
Endlessly made pure

In the quiet exhumation
Of an unlived life, drawn
Moth-like to the light?

II

Old bones rattle
In the carcasses
Of old lives.

Bodies at dusk
Creak with the chill
Of forgotten stones.

Black worms bore
The moonlit earth
In search of food.

III

Once a year
A mirror breaks
A face dissolves

Seed pods burst
And find the earth
Strewn with life.

CHANCE MEETING

The restless intensity in your eyes
Your beard uncertain of its true length
Or shape, uneasiness underneath
Our banter about old times

I try to put your soul and skin together
Without much success. One of them is too
Well-ordered. The other spontaneously
Unraveling and regenerating itself
Defying orders to stay put.

TO THE OLD MAN FROM MILFORD

Go silently into the dark
Fields of a moonless night
Awaiting the rising of the Pleiades
Or sighting the double star in Cygnus.

Go lightly into the mist
Of mornings by the old stump
Where we collected puffballs big as pumpkins
And skipped stones along the shallow stream.

Go silently and you will hear
Sounds not yet untinged by fear
The lapping waves of a newly formed lake
Covering all memories in their wake.

Go lightly and you will feel
What time would have us both conceal
What once was lost without a trace
Regained in memories' failing grace.

ANASAZI

I have walked on your mesas
Played in your ball courts
And prayed by your kivas

But not with your fullness
Still lingering silently
In the desert dance
Of wind and light.

While others look for your dead
I see your living images
Rising through the sipapu.

Gentle Anasazi
May my footsteps
Consecrate the earth
As yours did.

HANUMAN

Mystic monkeys march in time

Enchained eternal recurrent rhyme

Celestial servants successively

Know now to know not, but to be.

DAYBREAK AT BROWNBACKS

All things, my father, must pass
Folded in the shrouded form
Of a poet's inner sense
The future resembles the past
Only in the quaint equations
Of slumbering physicists.

All things, my father, go into the past
Branches of the dying willow tree
Cover the ground, break underfoot
Slip back to brown-black earth
While a few green leaves
Reach for a blue-gray sky.

All things, my father, await the future
The dying tree trembles in the storm
The dead sleep, fearing judgment
As silence follows thunderclaps
Leaving no judgment on the new day
Unreborn, unrekindled, unremitting.

All things, my father, return to the present
Finding the place of each beginning
Before the beginning and after the end
Only eternity remains
Casting frozen images
That time cannot endure.

DIALECTIC

Barely attending to the day
The Owl of Minerva begins its flight
At evening, on the edge of space.

SERENITY

The tree-shuttered path
Scatters sunlight into shadows
The indifferent chaos of the sun
Is diffused, altered by the
Dance of darkness and light
Where the patterns of presence
Need only the truth of the visible.

The path beckons. I follow.
Even the oldest gods of earth
Do not know I passed this way,
And was at peace.

APPEARANCES

The gray cathedral Notre Dame
Welcomes late winter's children in
From out of heaven's time
Behind the mask of form sublime
Where all begin to feel the rhyme
And rhythm in the calm
Allude to visions unforeseen
Where objects are not what they seem.

A child sleeps in summer colors
Gray beginnings blown away
By bright blues and white
Clouds that mottle the moon at night
By day keeping the sun from sight
While green shimmerings in August heat
Allude to visions unrefined
Keep the earth-eye in the mind.

STILL LIFE

Gather into yourself
the living and the dead.
Everything born becomes
dust, dreams, and decay.

I picked flowers today
and laid them on your table.

OPPOSITION

The pure open texture of the full moon
Greets the rose-fingered clouds
Of a pastel sunrise
Softening, for a moment
The sequestered sense
Of precarious life.

FOUND POEMS

In forgotten boxes in the attic
In forgotten words of the sixties
Images of Yeats, Pound and Eliot
Embellished with Eastern mysteries

Creep into my hands. They ask,
Do you remember us? We are
Here for the Second Coming. For the
Thought and theory which you have

Forgotten. So I watched
That hour as it passed
Beneath the cold sun
Of a winter mind beholding
Nothing that was there
Something that wasn't.

WRITER'S BLOCK

The struggle is not with words or meanings
    and still less with the self (for
    none of it is personal.)

Instead it is with this: the fly
    that buzzes on forever
    and will not land, the one

We will not swat, for fear the world
    will explode. Or implode.
    Depending on our choice
    of elements. Or characters.

CONSTRUCTIONS IN ONE DIMENSION

The point at infinity
Vanishes in the perfect circle

The material of the past
Vanishes in the form of the future

The death of the parent
Vanishes in the life of the child

A WHIMSICAL ONTOLOGY

The only thing that makes us think

that this
      and that
            are there:

if all this
      were that
            and all that this

then we would be nowhere.

WALLACE STEVENS
AT THE BARBEQUE

The trees were large

The mind was small

The rest did not

Matter.

MEMOIR OF A GIRL WHO LOST HER LIFE SHADOWBOXING IN GRIFFITH PARK

for Carol Brown

I am
   an innocent victim
      in my war
         with myself,
            waged against
               the possibility of being,
               an intangible thing.

BALING HAY IN VALLEY FORGE

October slips in behind summer in these parts.
He saw it coming in September, while
August haze still lingered with cool breezes
and warm sun. A cusp on the edge of time.
Neither the brilliant blue of the sky,
nor the faded green of the trees, nor the
rustling of the leaves in the quiet breeze,
belonged to any season.

He felt the universe in his hands.
Would he choose to turn it back to summer,
not the sultry, debilitating summer
infecting his memory, but a perfect summer
where warmth brought forth life, new and
invigorating? Or forward to autumn,
breathtaking in its harvest, bringing
new clarity to earth and sky, and hope,
hope for a peaceful year?

Choose he could, but stay he could not.
For the moment was not in time, not moving
as the side rake moved, piling up one row of hay
next to another. It stood as each row stood,
apart. He tried to stay, but time returned
him as a blade of grass, and the baler
took him on his way.

ALONG THE WISSAHICKON

Blue sky after a night rain.
It seemed as if right action
Might be enough, as if pain
Could be, at least, discounted.

These yellow gleanings seemed
To glide along the earth:

A tree-disguised snake
Shed its skin along the trail.
A black dog splashed
In the creek. A woman
In a red vest mounted
An uprooted tree trunk.

A warm yellow sun,
Glistening on the rapids,
Freed his mind from
The cold dawn.

DURING A LULL IN THE FIGHTING

As a bald man shaves his head
To conceal his baldness
Memory erases the past
To conceal the present.

The life of the dead
Is in the past: they
do not live on but back,
back in remembered time
where we create
our future.

I have made
the dangerous passage
between the world
without objects and
the one with.

But I will not live
to tell about it.

RAID ON THE INARTICULATE

We learn to survive
Keep it to ourselves
Carefully cloaked
In dissimilitude

Mr. Wittgenstein's duck-rabbit terrifies us in its openness

The man waking in the morning survives
In the man asleep at night, or dies.
But that is not the same as.....

the lost
memory of the wind
or

the recurring
dream of spring
or

the distant sounds
of birds in summer

.....the white emptiness outside time.

SEARCH FOR A METHOD

She found strange patterns on the old wall
Where the old kitchen cabinets once stood
Before she made renovation the order of the day.

The faded orange and yellow colorings
Framed by broken lines of smokey dust
Etched themselves into her mind
In tones that only time could make
That restoration would destroy.

Perhaps that was why she attacked
The wall with such vengeance
In her quest for the perfectly exposed brick.
The crumbling plaster dust carried
Memories in Brownian motion
Random walks, randomly downward
To the dustpan casket on the floor.

THE DESIRE TO LIVE IN THE PRESENT

A backward glance to catch
the thief of stones stealing
the rocks from the river

Lost again
the great greek god goes west
as the sun sets.

So now he is another man
a man we all knew
yesterday.

The axe severs the root
dawn breaks
on a new day.

To find you in a foreign land
shopping for trinkets
in a draughty church.

Where does it end, this day?
Will I have time to find it?

THE QUIET DRUM

The moon followed her at night
As it had when she was a child
When trees reflected on the lake
Were ghosts no words could dispel
Now the shadows no longer spoke
Quietly, fearfully, to the inner ear
No ideas lingered in the firelight
And the only forms
Were the cold forms
Of darkness.

She knew that yesterday's ghost
Had vanished in today's sunlight.
She knew there were children asleep
On the other side of the world.
But in the warmth of an afternoon sun
When the ancient terror returned
She knew the mind was not appeased
By reason. It had to be assaulted
Brutalized, struck dumb
Before she could listen
To the primitive silence
Trapped in the trees.

THE SUN SETS EVERY DAY

Steel gray symbols: the sky,
the bridge, and the Susquehanna.

The river and the rose
rise in the sky,
burning still as you nibble
around the edge of your sandwich,
failing to attack the central morsel,
the bite into the depths of darkness.

So you fall down into your book,
reading poetry at nightfall,
as a suicide leaps from the bridge
washed seaward
into the endless ocean.

EMERGING FROM THE TUNNEL

The treetops have been trimmed.

It tells us to proceed
          with the war.

We gather up the radishes,
     some onions,
an occasional rutabaga,
     and hurl them
     at the enemy.

He is unmoved.

Hunkered down behind the hedgerow,
waiting for the white rose,
amid the blood of earth our home,
we deny burial to the dead
in earth the eternal tomb.

Now they return
     seeking release
          in our suffering.

SECONDARY PROPERTIES

Today the day
does not need the night
and truth does not
need falsehood.
Old railroad cars collect here and tell
their travel stories:
the frozen nights in Montana
the sweltering heat of Arizona in summer
the sleepless nights carrying coal
and returning empty.

The fading sun brightens fall colors
in forests punctuated by power lines.
Clouds turn the sky
into a pastel postcard.
A sunset half-moon winks at the day
and disappears.

I am followed by the moon,
the sun,
the forests.
They want to convince me
they will be here
when I am gone.
But I know better.
When I sleep they disappear
when the night comes
the day recedes.
When I go
I take the colors with me.

The Hangman's Songs

..... de tous tes conseils l'univers est absent.

Gerard de Nerval
Vers Dores

I

I have come to break the stone
Break the stone and be alone
In the rocks I think I see
Sculpture of infinity.

Break again, break until
You have shown you have the will
Of nothingness and dust.

Will the race die from the weight
Of the dead who stay up late
To drink the living dry? Or flow
On until some sun has changed
Dead memories into living flames
As we with one another's children go?

II

There is no eye
Behind the mind
No place to make
The unseen soul
unwind. Or else

What thought have we
In this age found
To run a battleship aground
To keep an emperor from sin
Or bring the daily forage in.

Do not sing the song so well
That we cannot from heaven tell
The earth where we must live
Dream's perfection cannot be wrought
In sunlight without shadow's thought.

III

At your peril you deny
Daily death when you decry
The solace of the sun.

Along the path you must clip-clop
Without the power of the crop
Or spur. Dig in: the ride is long
And will come back into the gray
Of evening and the black
Of night.

The wine of earth is blood
And tears the words of death
Cry now, my pretty one
Cry now upon the grave of death
And bury him.

IV

I have not found a way to take
Away a life and leave no wake
Now by churchyard graves I see
Stone mirrors of what I might be
On each a name without a face
On each a time about a place
Where someone lived or died.

I once walked upon a ground
Where few men walk, I heard a sound
Devoid of color, timbre, tone
Then I knew I was alone
But for a cat of silent feet
Who followed me on each retreat
To hear my silent cries.

But silent feet and golden eyes
Won't listen to my deadly lies
Words I tell myself at night
Of how I do not mean to kill
Why I always lack the will
To turn and run in fright.

With my sins forever scarred
Body's death will be no guard
What savior can save me now
Or at least show me how
To whistle through the graveyard
When the cats are on the prowl?

V

You who think you will be free
In substance and reality
Will be shackled to a life
Where stolen shadows must suffice.

Stolen from the silent time
Where I learned to make my rhyme
Cold steel ax head in my hand
Try and take it, if you can.

You who lack the will to know
Will find you have nowhere to go
Unless you learn to pay the price
Stolen shadows must suffice.

VI

History will come round again
History will come round
The rope is tight
The walker walks
History will come round.

Bacon fat and kidney pie
Newton in the mind's eye
Forward travelers to your goal
Wealth of nations growing old.

Return, return, you will not learn
All before the beginning was
History will come round again
History will come round
After the end you will discern
Still points where nothing ever turns.

Children in some spring in June
Will enter life in full bloom
Sixteen candles will you light
And they will set the world aright.

History will come round again
History will come round
The rope will break
The walker fall
And history will come round.

VII

The train is going down the track
When will the train be coming back
I saw it going out of sight
And went to school so that I might
Learn midnight is a game we play
But midnight never comes.

A man is buried in the ground
And then he never makes a sound
So we, the living, think
Is midnight just a game we play
Where midnight never comes?

We live in a time of many dictums
Of wars without innocent victims
There is no other way
For midnight is a game we play
But midnight never comes.

From your body you have rent
Eyes of a beaming innocent
So this is where the cities went:
Boring suburbs, bitter slums
And midnight just a game to play
Where midnight never comes.

Now we've got it down to this:
That reason is emotionless
Time's arrow points in just one way
Leaving but little time to play
That midnight game we always lose
For midnight we can never choose.

VIII

Time has gone and time has come
Until our daily bread is done
Broken men just sit and sit
On gallows grounded on their wit
Treesouls sundered by the wind
Sundered by the wind.

I made my peace with Uncle Sam
With all the people of the land
Then had a dream just yesterday
Of a child on barren earth at play
When all the trees were gone away
When all the trees were gone.

Now seasons season ends
And leaves no longer fall
Eternal life must make amends
While tree trunks heed the call
And go to find another home
To find another home.

IX

The old ways are no more, no more
The old ways are no more
For youth has gone to war with age
And ages yet to come
In conscious impotence of rage
Hopeless mortals on the run.

Go away, oh go away, oh
Go away from here
Listen not to what they say
But listen to their fear
Wolves are howling in the wind
Howling in the wind.

Again the words the frozen words
Recur eternally
Cast in that broken form of life
That youth alone can see
Old men without the hope of kin
Without the hope of kin.

X

Green September sings a song
Spring a memory, summer gone
I never see a setting sun
Never end what I've begun
Since I lost the sound of trees
Lost the sound of trees.

December will not come this year
But with a trembling and a fear
That shakes a cold hard earth
And empties all of any worth
For I have lost the sound of trees
I have lost the trees.

January will remake
The world I see at each daybreak
Bring back a summer-setting day
But life is what I'll need to pay
Until I see the sound of trees
Until I see the sound.

XI

All of life
All of death
Will not make us whole.

Time alone
Will soon reshape
Our never-ending goal.

Another Life

Qué hace una mosca encarcelada
en un soneto de Petrarca?

> Pablo Neruda
> *Question Book*

To imagine a language.....
...... is to imagine a form of life

> Ludwig Wittgenstein
> *Philosophical Investigations*

SHORELINES

Others have come before and written
What I can see but cannot say
Still, I return, like a sea to its shore
To search among the pebbles of the beach
For some pure form of poetry

It must be pure yet consummate
In evil and in good
Leaving nothing out.

It must never show
Its footsteps.

SPRING LIGHT

Cold spring dulls the subtle sense

Of early evening light

In a life unwound by winter

Opened out again

To children's laughter

Bringing life to dreams

And dreams to life.

THE END OF SOMETHING

In your hands
The '36 Desoto
Winds along
Saw Mill River Parkway
Darts out
The No Merge Exit
Exiting

To Pleasantville and
Your brother's garden.
We pull weeds
(without gloves)
Making room for
Potatoes and dinner.
Dirty fingernails
(you say without speaking)
Are part of the joy
That holds us to earth.

Now I know
What you knew then.
We all die
With a little
Bit of dirt
Under our nails.

A SECOND SON

I look back
Holding the old
Photograph and feel
Your words come back
Marveling at how many
I thought were mine.

This was your gift
The song you left
The quiet words
On late nights
On long weekends
Strangely soft
For all the hard
Edges and sharp points
Pinning me
To reality in spite
Of myself.

No matter
What song
I sing
I cannot
Return the gift
Cannot make
A wish
A father
To a deed
That can't
Be done.

No poem
Without price
Would penetrate
The grave
Of a dead poet
Silent now
And cold.

And yet.

Your words that lived
Are living
In me now
Carried many years
In ways
I did not know
Returning from
Foreign places where
Phantom memories go
A web of words
Spread far and wide
Spanning living
Things and dead
Connect the quiet evening
To a day that's
Filled with dread.

And all the words
That stumble forth
From the chaos of the sun
Contain the father's light
However hard and lonely
The new life that's been won.

SOLITARY CONVERSATIONS

You said: the present is place
Without description, time
Without words and hence
The only time we share
With the trees.

Perhaps the earth too
Moves in this time
Immemorial, ever present
In the slow songs
Of rumbling volcanoes.

You put it there, old friend
That element of earth
For me to break these words on
The sediment of conversation
Unwritten, unwritable.

Tell me, was that why Plato saw
A poverty in written words
Desiring the pure forms
Found in the face

Of another face
Keeping the thought
That flickers in the eye
Unseen by anyone
Alone.

MILFORD SPRING

A father took his son one day on a long car ride
Through rolling hills and valleys: they loved the countryside
They stopped the car beside the road and looked down from the ridge
In apple blossom fields they saw a barn-red covered bridge.
A hidden path led from the ridge, through green fields and morning mists
A fragrant journey to the bridge, full of turns and twists
Across the bridge a hollow sound of footsteps on the wood
Who would know that over there so vast a meadow stood!

Stretched before them everywhere were fields and barnyard scenes
Fields of wheat and timothy, and freshly flowing streams.
The people looked surprised to see these strangers in their midst
They looked as if they'd never known an outer world exists.
Farmers there in Milford Mills with cows and goats and pigs
Wearing old-time overalls, riding tractors slow and big
Pulling bumpy wagons loaded high with bales of hay
Loaded all by hand in a plain old-fashioned way.

The people came to farm the land many years ago
Became a memory to the world whose ways they did not know.
Everyone went by so fast they never saw the way.
The father found the land at peace and made his plans to stay.
His son longed to see the world again, for he had much to learn
And so he left and headed west, sure he could return.
His memory was so clear it seemed the path could not be lost
He never stopped to think there could ever be a cost.

Years later he returned to find his way
Through country lanes and fields of hay
Where once the road had led
But this time on the hilltop he stopped dead
To see a lake with little boats
Gone were the cows, the sheep, the goats
Now sadly did he turn around
To see the spring, once underground
Now turned to water everywhere
And wondered whether heaven had been spared.

SUNRISE AT SLIGO CREEK

The birds know it's time
To respect the quiet majesty
Of another day
Slight shivers in the night
Sense something on the way.

Dawn breaks through the woods
Like a child growing up
Treetop shrouds of darkness
Come alive with light
All in one sip from my cup.

Now the day has come
But its visit will be brief
For its job is never done:
Sunlight seldom strikes
Both sides of the leaf.

A LONG STORY

Now you dream
and come to see
the great fear
of knowing where
the road leads

Knowing that knowing
must reject itself
and live only
in a generation
of innocence

Where death is
no more natural
than life, no more
than the possibility
of another life

Taken from stones
washed clean
in the canals
of a dead city

Kissed by dreams
of life.

LOOKING FOR ITALIAN BRANDY IN THE FRENCH QUARTER

Edging into bitterness

Breaking through broken clouds

Like a half moon in the mist

Made all too clear

By memories of the Via Delarosa

I ask for the only form

Of forgiveness I can find --

A pilgrimage to the

Cafe Du Monde.

AN UNEXPECTED SUNRISE
Mt. Tamalpais Cemetery
January 25, 1997

Water falls in torrents
Over sun-sprinkled rocks
Past the grasses blown
by coastal breezes
Past the green moss
on the grey stone
Into the cemetery culvert.

While the dead stand guard
With their flowers and flags.

All this will change
Except the cascading sounds
Ancient and unrepeatable.

PALM TREES AND POSSIBILITIES

In a morning meditation
Limited only by light
And other absolutes
She accepted her choice
Of infinities: to go along
The old way, *und so weiter*
Or cut across
Along the line laid out
By Pythagoras & the paradoxes
Of the modern world.

DAYFIRE

Uncertain sense
Of place broken
By distant breakers

Morning fire
Delicate as light
Filtered through
Trees at dawn

Afternoon dreams
In blue sky ravaged
By unseen thunders
Raging storms

Evening floats
In quiet distance
Autumn dayfires
Lost in winter ice

OLMEC COLOSSAL HEAD

What struggle is there
in these stones, what
sweet illusion of the heart
in every breath
thrown away
into life,
the abyss?

THE DEATH OF A MINOR MORRIS

I remember the turtle
   Running (turtle fashion)
   Across the mountain road
   With the world on its back.

And the driver
   Avoiding the turtle
   Leaving the road
   & the world
   behind.

THE ONTOLOGY OF LOST MOMENTS

Finally it was time to take the bull by the horns
To shake free from the unexpected influence of old anxieties
And look back over all those things I had just glanced at
Only lately beginning to bubble in the corner of the page.

At first it was hard living with the animals
Waking up with no one to talk to, recalling
Photographs, fleeting images, scraps of paper and other
Indifferent clues that the past is more than a memory.
Or an invention designed to ward off a few stubborn thoughts
That keep suggesting God doesn't take time seriously.

It was easy to forget the striking resemblance we bear to our ancestors
And how remote is any precise knowledge of just how this species began
The divide remains unknown & the circularity of the whole question
Imposes itself on us; we learn to live with the consequential doubt
And still remain unruffled underneath. Only then do we recognize
The road we once crossed before we were human and knew outselves.

I had been thinking about it for a long time
But still the ontology of lost moments
Was not quite what I had expected.
Additions to the stock of available reality
Proved as elusive as ever

My dad used to say that his mom used to say
"Be a good boy and keep your shoulders up,"
So he always kept his shoulders up. Some things are clear
I guess, even if the connections, whatever they were, are lost
So there's hope. But we've got to start somewhere
Away from the flush of time that always seems to
Define the core of the argument where we never expected it
And certainly never planned when we put the building up.

Bathrooms are nearly always near elevators. Stairs too.
Marginal notes matter. Dust accumulates around all the old words
The thin clear lines so alive in the characters of yesterday's argument
Have grown whiskers in today's language. It's not clear anymore
Where the center is and how we're supposed to get hold of it.

Our interior devotions don't quite measure up
Without some kind of outward criterion. But
When you think about it, everything can't all
Be in the performance and even illocutionary
Utterances can turn suicidal if you're not careful.
All in all maybe it's better to keep to yourself
And not give too much away, at least not without
Receiving adequate compensation.

It's going to take more work getting the effort put
In the right place instead of always missing the target
And ending up having to start the thing all over again.
We get paid all right but how long can things go on like this?
One piece of paper here or there won't matter but in time
Everything does. It all adds up if you are willing
To do the calculation which, I can see, you're not.

I plan to tell you about it when I get a chance to sit
Down and find the words. Write a letter maybe
Quaint as that seems under the circumstances
Dinner will be late. No, not again, remember
Last night we ate at Pizza Hut and spilled the beer
And got home late anyway so it all seems to end up
In the same place no matter where we start but it's
Not easy to tell because it seems we're always starting
Something new and still losing track of where we set
Out from. Am I making sense? I guess not. *Time*
For bed, anyway, and we've got a lot to do tomorrow.

I can't seem to sit and concentrate with all this racket
Buzzing around inside my head, if that's where it is.
Sorry, I was distracted, may I help you with something?
No, we're out today, but you can try again tomorrow.
It's always been there, I suppose, but who has time
To pay that much attention to it with everything else
Yes, I know, you came a long way, but really there's
Nothing I can do about it but give you a rain check.
That you have to plan for these days. I don't know
Why things have to work that way but they do. Modern times,
I guess. *I could set one aside and give you a call*
If that would help. Good. Sorry I can't do more.

It all feels backwards. And that would be OK
Except we have to begin at the beginning
And never be quite sure where the end is.
Maybe we don't even know, after all, where the beginning is
And we're just stuck, captive to Pascal's two infinities
Or trapped like Marlowe, breathing dead hippo meat
And leaving the rest to devils and angels. But I've got to say
Literature won't help much and philosophy won't either
When you sit cross-legged somewhere in the middle
Of the Western tradition.

Here in the states we live on a borrowed tongue
We brought from the old world along with the sheep
And probably never quite molded to the new demands
Of the frontier. Sometimes we come up short, looking
For a word in someone else's language. We never get to know
Where it came from in the first place but I guess that's
To be expected since it's their language
That we just picked up and didn't change much
At least not like they did. So it's hard to find out
What the voice of America really is.

We fell into the furrows of some great thought
Then sprouted up, speaking first in tongues
And then tying it all together in what
Looked like a language but remained
Only audible pauses in a silent ether.
In the old days before portable phones
This left us time for a coffee break or a drink
Now everything is chatter and infoglut and
High-tech talk. Still, leaves fall every year
And serve as sort of a symbol of the insignificance
Of symbols, human or otherwise. Not that this
Nullifies anything, since there are plenty of symbols
Around perfectly capable of blowing their own horns
Pointing to sources of our own significance, many of them
Polluted even if we've been lately cleaning up our act.

Part of this began before we were born
But we will never know which. It's too
Hard to look back that far, past the invention
Of self, the one that kept us alive but sometimes
Seems to have cost too much. We never gather
Evidence about the benefits without shaking the picture
And having everything go out of focus just when
We begin to feel like we're getting somewhere.
I don't want to overplay this: each breath is evidence
That we are on the right track or are at least
Perpetually willing to wait and find out more
About how the accounting really works.

We live with the necessity of keeping our own accounts
And won't be judged by the magnitudes but only by
The absolute value of something quite immeasurable
Yet still not entirely beyond calculation even though
The rules are private and not all of our own making.

Everything is what it is and not some other thing.
An idea is like nothing but an idea.
These have been replaced in our century
By our growing awareness of how words work
And new developments in brain chemistry.

NORTH & SOUTH

We all go through phases, I guess
right now mine is this:
the spare lines of philosophy
crowd out the careful chaos
of poetry. That is, until each line
becomes short by its own measure,
the internal necessity of being only
what it is, the straight and narrow
way without end through the
crisscross constantly cut short
by time. And death. The death
of a line, ever present in its endpoints
holds it back everywhere
except in the inner lives of certain persons
where infinity lives as a constant
shower of light over the dark
quilt of time.

AGAINST TIME

Only through time is time conquered.

T.S.
Eliot

Light in the East

Poetry comes ..... when no longer thinking about it.

Lu Yu

MORNING

Moonlight on the fruit basket
Sunlight in the trees
In an uneasy silence
A cat breathes

OUT WEST: THE SALT RIVER

Sun down, radio off
Rolling down the canyon,
Road echoes make
A hallowed ground of change
Where life keeps emerging out of death
Where stones speak across the centuries
Where light keeps appearing in the east
Bearing Erebus backwards
Into chaos
Of night
Of day
Of unrelenting
Time.

THE OCEAN HAS NO NAME

We were always outsiders
In a quiet place of no beginnings,
A corner where the waves came up
And the salt spray dissolved our thoughts
In the midst of a cycle only the sea knows
As it strips the land of its shorelines
Tearing our nets, tossing up our losses
Without measure.

EARLY RAIN,
MORNING CLOUDS

Wind outside
A quiet house
Shakes green leaves
In early spring.

Brown wood of winter
Stands in stillness

Silence breaks
A heating fan speaks
The forced air
Of winter.

THE WORLD AS PHOTOGRAPH

Yesterday's rain brushes away
The blemished air brooding
Around the trees and under
The gray afternoon's nightlikeness
Touching us with blue
Indifference to the darker cares
Of a three day's rain that hemmed us
In too deeply to our own
Interior wandering on an earth
Dark and rumbling as an underworld.

Did we take it all too much to heart?
Or did we fear the joy of light
Breaking through with the false
Purity of a picture postcard?
Next time we will wait longer
For the world without the photograph
But with the touch of light
Relieved of pure rationality
Packaged and loosed upon the world
By digital dreams of untempered
Turing machines taking away
The cold press of granite reality.

TRANSCENDENCE IN BLUE & GREEN

Not for one time only
Or for all
But for the very idea
That there might be time

For wondering where the lost
Texas summer goes
Scampering away
With horned toads and
Armadillo's dust
Hanging in the air.

Or hanging on words
Floating on pure
Mediterranean breezes
Sunlight unfiltered in
Blue green oils
On painter's canvas
Still moving outward
Textured in time
Mindrops making
The journey out and in
Out and in.

CORNFIELD AT NIGHT

That summer we planted corn
And hid among the stalks in fall
Until the moon came out
So we could walk
Out of the darkness
Of a daytime self
With rainy thoughts
And go quietly
Down a dustless road
While moonlight moved
Approaching midwinter.

AUTUMN DUST

The dry summer left us
With a thirst unquenchable
By the wine growing in the grapes
Or aging in the barrels.

We searched for some deeper satisfaction
In the colors of falling leaves
But found mostly browns and yellows
Not the greater brilliance we had hoped for.

So we settled for the taste
of last year's wine
And danced away
the dwindling light
In a carnival of dead leaves
and laughing children.

LATE FALL

Red leaves fooled us that year
Bursting from behind the mask
Of brown and yellow
As unexpected as
The colors in your voice, or
The unspoken softness in your lips
Untouched by mine yet touched
In a mind not quite my own.

LOVE'S CONDENSATE

Yesterday's poems are lost
In yesterday's yearning
Unrequited by today's desire.

I look at you
As close to me
As the time light takes
To travel to the eye
Or touch to tremble
In the brain.
Today's poem
Brings you
Closer
......Still.

CONTROLLED BURNING

Yellow and red
Sun and blood
Outer and inner
Flame around
White hot blue
Eyes inside
Another world
Where words
Are the flesh
Of our bodies
Speech the steam
In the bedroom
Of desire.

ABOVE CAESAR'S HEAD

The carpet flamed in quick
pools of blue, unyellowed
proof that the white-mule
bore only water of life.

But I, in doubt of fire,
with salt dispelled it,
while others, natives
hailing the test, exulted.

Later the headlights,
hunting the mountain road
froze cold knives in fog.

CAESAR'S HEAD REVISITED

The trees stand like legions
Against the force of time
Taking and giving empires

Wearing their clouds
Like little white caps
Of smoke still rising
From a battle mixed
In the blood of history
And future time.

BARN WORK

Sometimes he would hover
Over a point of some returning
When his memory buried other
Stops along his journey
Where fiction carried stories
His facts could not foresee
And his acts brought back
Silent sacred worries
His words could not redeem.

Then the smell of rotting things
(A hayloft in high summer,
Cow pastures in early morning)
Cornered his desire
For paradise and bound him
To an earth he could not choose
Not to be part of.

Until the light became longer
With the days' expanse
Sultry in a summer balance
Beginning a pattern in slow
Time moving back near
An unmoved fear, a stony
Time sliding slowly
Along the moon's trace
Tracking through tunnels
Laid softly down
In lost languages.

CROSSCURRENTS

Raindrops falling on the screen
Walk like crabs across the sand
Following pathways unforeseen
Pirates carrying contraband

The word wanders in regret
Prisoner on the printed page
Lost in a language we forget
As soon as the ink begins to age.

TRANSFORMATION

Language may be tyranny
A prison of syntax
And deep structures
Imagined in our genes
Giving life only
To dead letters.

Or language
May be freedom
Dancing beyond us
In pictograms overlain
With letters leaving behind
Yesterday's dreamless nights,
Like shackles left
On a prison floor
Of wordlessness.

REMEMBRANCE

The quiet pull
of unknown dreams
in darkly forming hills
the moon in the mountains
breaks the stillness of a Chinese jar
in a world of ten thousand things
ten thousand words at nightfall
won't keep the pale moonlight
from sensing silent sorrows
at the center of the heart.

ART FILM

In dark time
We searched mind-scattered
Contents of emptied pockets
Purses and broken cases
Abandoned and lost
Along the way.

Flakes of fresh snow
Falling as we left the movie
Found the lucky penny
We held on to but thought lost.

THE PLACE OF SOLITUDE
WHERE THREE DREAMS CROSS

She hid among the trees
And walked through the forest
As night brought the curtain down
On happiness, her voice
Calling from the trees
Touching her outside to my inside
Falling on my stony silence.
Was it fear that brought us together
Or love of something
Other than ourselves, looking
For the clearing in the woods
Where the pumpkin in the garden
The iridescence of a waterfall at noon
Live inside us, pulling us
Toward daylight.

LOVERS' QUESTIONS

How do I see
The silence in the colors
Of your voice?

How do I taste
The sadness in the sound
Of your smile?

How do I devour
The emptiness of the space
Between us?

DREAM SHADOWS

Late afternoon carries the day

Through fields where lovers stay

Along a winding twilight road

     Of golden leaves.

We land in one another's arms

And tumble through the corners

     In our lives.

We are and are not

There and not there

Shadows in each others'

     Fallen dreams.

TAKOMA STATION

Love is hardest
Steel against blue sky
All else pales before it
As many gods pale
Before one. Bright light
Splits black clouds
Of uncovered positions
At the center
Of the pyramid.

A pastel morning breaks
A night's dark foreboding
Clouds mellow only in the mind

The poem came first
Then the day without pattern
Light indirect in the tumid air
That exists always and everywhere
Before the trees and the buildings
And cars and buses and finally
The people placed judiciously
Behind the steering wheels.

CAR TALK

Gray day
Drifting fog
Maybe
Even the BMWs
Will stay home

Moving West

The harp of Pythagoras goes on resonating in the silence.
Antonio Machado

VIA NEGATIVA

A poem is not an example
From any theory of poetry.

That
Is what makes it
A poem.

CESAR VALLEJO: REFLECTIONS ON A MANUSCRIPT

I, yes, even I
Child of the father of the new
Pounded out poems
In Courier type
Fixed points on now
Faded paper
And crossed them out
In giant, angry scrawls
That howled beyond the power
Of any words I wrote:
I could never hit the keys
Hard enough to push my letters
Through the hole in life
Drawn by death.

TURNER AT LARGE

If words were all we had
to paint a silent Turner sea
the darker and the lighter parts
the moon's pull, that slow
undertow of eternal tides
the sea would keep all its secrets
and words could not unlock
the sea that seethes inside us
like a mad lost buffalo's plunge
from a cliff

      to the rocks

         to the sea.

MEROVINGIAN MEMORY

*It was in the face of the miraculous
that they became most human.*
R.W. Southern
*The Making of the
Middle Ages*

Come, my queen, and see
The unfolding of the light of heaven
God's promise brought before our eyes
Our courtyard brilliant with a glow
Greater than any you have seen.

Look away, look away forever
From the burning sky-fire
That sears your eyes
And freezes you in sin.

Now, my lord, tell me
By what right have you read
Fear into the blood-red rain
Come from the sky
To cure my sins
Of their virgin birth.

PHIDIAS AT NIGHT

Shadows in sunlight
Sharp and clear
Cut the heart.

Shadows in the fire
Break the will
Of a terracotta army.

Ladder on the wall
To nowhere, let me
Climb your shadow
To the sky

Into the night
Where shadows sculpt
A new day out of
Moonlight's dust.

ADMONITION FOR THE NEW DAY

After H.M.

I ask you
What is the shape of the dawn
The red one, the angry
Azimuth of the day?
What thread am I
In this long rope of days?
And who but you
Will pull me along
Through the mud-soaked mornings
The dust-borne afternoons
Or evening's slow titration
Of light fading on the page
Moving beyond the poetry
A foreign language written
By the clouds' cadence
The shadowy rhythm of light
Against descending darkness
As the days drop
Out of sight?

We are a battleground
Without armies
A crusade with only
A mission,
Pillaging
The countryside of time
In search of an absolute end.
We make the day lurch forward
Toward an Armageddon of the mind
Carrying a warning
As night becomes morning
And I unravel
The skein of my time
Into yours, drawing up
Our bill of particulars
Against the reigning kingdom
Of recurring night

SAPPHO OUT OF TIME

The singer never saw
this song she sang
never saw her sound
move in the moods
of minds beyond
her voice

Where fragments fill
with new forms filtered
by the slow decay of time
and Alexandrian papyrus
as we make our own
words from words
she never knew.

SCHOLARS AT DINNER

We are all Sappho's children
Carrying gifts to her gods
Mixing memory and desire
To burn her unburnt offering
To sing her unsung songs
And bring back bright love
From the black earth of war

We are all Sappho's children
Dreamers awake at midnight
Inventing words for her songs
Garlands for the untouched
Islands in the passions
Of our modern minds

We are all Sappho's children
Filling in holes in our lives
Fragments of forgotten poems
Broken shards of semi-conscious
Songs once sung and now
Unsung except when unremembered.

THE BATTLE OF SALIMAS

Life is not breath
Or moments between
Inhaling and exhaling
Or any place in time,
It is the saving of the city
The bending of the oar
Against the ocean
And the enemy
The holding of everything
For one life
Lived in one moment
Collapsed in an interior
Devotion to begin
What no one
Can complete.

PLATO'S GHOST

•

•

•

•

There's your life
Laid out under glass
It's a gift: open it.

RECOLLECTIONS

Stepping Stones
(Poems in Transition)

Divinity must live within herself.

Wallace Stevens
Sunday Morning

ALTE MUSÍK
For an Old Friend Leaving Vienna

It is old, this Vienna
The one the Romans left
Behind in the bones of soldiers
Under a city of dreams.

You came with such hope
To touch and hold some secret
Purchased with an emperor's fortune
And locked away, captured
In palaces and picture frames.

Of course you had so little time
(One week! How foolish!
What could you hope to find?)
Time to seek a skeleton
Of a life, nothing more.

You leave with a sense of sadness
At having left so much undone
At having unlocked so little
Of the secret in yourself.

Except at times when you still hear
Old music from the Ruprechskirche
And know how long you will see
Something of yourself in the life
Of this Vienna you are leaving.

TERMS AND CONDITIONS

I watched the embers of a life
In the headlights of a dream
And watched the rabbit run
Under the wheel of fortune.

That day the dawn broke
Down a delicate balance
Between dream and desire.

You spoke to me and said,
"Nothing comes out of the past
But everything goes
Into the future."

CROSSING THE WATER

We took rocks
to dam the creek
and make the water
deep enough
to swim in
losing forever
the stepping stones
we followed as children
crossing the stream
to pick wild
dreams.

ACROSS THE THRESHOLD

Touch me
In the deep
Unspoken emptiness
I leave at your door
And let me enter
Your community without words
Unmade flesh
On an unmade bed
There to be molded
Around the idea of a body
In the body of ideas
We make in our touch
And touch in our making.

IN REASON'S SHADOW

Somewhere in the middle of today
I found a yesterday
Buried in the soft rock
Of a memory exquisitely carved
To obscure itself from view:
The dark side
Of an uncharted moon
Lost in the laws
Of perspective.

NIGHT TERROR

I am lost again
In the morning light
Of the day-long dawn
In green emptiness
Against the mass of night.

The time will come
When I no longer seek
To see the night
Stolen from the day,
To see the shroud of darkness
Returned to the terror
Of the night.

Then the night will be at peace
In me, and I will be at peace
In the night.

ON PURIFICATIONS

*In darkness they roam
over the meadow.*
Empedokles

Skip over the darkness

To the new light

Stones don't float

On the water

They root in the mantle

And float in the fire

Or rest quenched in the water

Of life-bringing earth.

FINAL SUN

Memory and reality must
be in one space.
Ludwig Wittgenstein
Philosophical Remarks

Morning wakes

Above the trees

Along Sligo Creek

To light this page.

Memory wakes

Above the trees

Along Marsh Creek

To move this pen.

[Sligo Creek: Silver Spring, MD, 2002

Marsh Creek: Milford Mills, PA, 1958]

MEASURE ZERO

A flickering light
Masks an outer darkness.

A single note
Sounds an inner silence.

Here is: everywhere.

The landscape of dreams
Has no extension.

ANOTHER LOOK

Another look behind
the waking self
and the sleeping:

> can you see
>
> the slow descent
>
> into senselessness?

Another look behind
the light moments
and the dark:

> can you move
>
> the blue clouds away
>
> from the dawn?

TOUCHING DOWN IN DENVER

The mountains are a cradle
For an earth-born god
Of a crimson sky that melts
At morning light.

I want to land there
In the trees and their forests
To hear the singing birds
Bring back old mornings
One more time.

But not now.......

We have hedged the heights of time
Smoothed out the sadness of valleys
And triumphed over
Our fear of mountain tops.

We fly over the idea of a mountain
And cancel the thought of a valley
So we can land on one level runway
And take off on another.

We are no longer foot-travelers of time,
Feeling old bones under our feet. How
Many ancient burial grounds have we missed
On this flight from the old to the new,
What shadows do the mountains cast
On the runways of our dreams, and what valley
Can survive the incessant harmony
Of a human mind bent on harnessing
Every hard-to-handle horse with a well
Measured martingale of time?

SILENCE OF THE LANDS

In a pool of memory a pebble drops
as the next war begins, and stops
for now.
Factions and rarefactions.
condensation and its discontents
swirl around the peripatetics
in my head.

The arguments back up into a corner
where infinity is the only way out.
I wait for some wind so the dry
winter cornstalks can crumble
back to earth.

Ridgelines

Poems and Afterthoughts

BLUE RIDER

I pass this on to those I ride with
Along the ridges of the mind
Where the future lies trapped
In the valley of my memory.

The past is a dead god
Frozen and crippled
I am its prisoner.

I will be saved by horses
Breaking through the cold dew
A stampede of chaos tamed
By lost memories waking
In the sun.

LAUREL FORK CREEK

Here I am on Sunday morning
Reading fragments of Archimedes
And poems of Charles Wright
Looking for ineffable connections

Asking what lies between
This Blue Ridge sunrise
A Buffalo Mountain sunset
And the slow shifting
Earthlight of late afternoon?

For me it starts with the same
Inevitable inability to say
What I want to say
Leaving only the desire
To let things of this world
Make themselves manifest.

SUN OVER PLYWOOD

The present sun ancient
As the morning light
Shows nothing less than
Chaos from a long
Night rain

Knots not made
By any hand
Pressed into place
As temporary shelter
From the cold

AND SO THE LIGHT GOES

Everything I know
Has started here
In the twilight
Of dreams
Lost and found.

And so the light goes

In and out
Yellow and orange
As blue-gray sky
Welcomes the day

So the light goes

On and off.
In the lighthouse
Of the mind.

LEAVING SANTA FE
(There Where I Am Not)

I am
In a fragment
Of Heraclitus
Consumed by fire
I am not here

I am
With the sail
Of Ulysses
Singing in the dark
I am not here

I am
With the flowers of evil
Tending my garden
On a drunken boat
I am not here

I am
In the mind of winter
Descending a mountain
Transported to summer
I am not here

I am
In a poem of Bei Dao
Chanting Tao Chien
At the sky's edge
I am not here

141

MARGINALIA

In the end the only sign
The scholar knows
is the sign itself.

Outside there is nothing,
Neither the wind in the trees
Nor the bright light of the sun
Nor the silent rumblings
Of the human heart.

Inside there remains
A cold eye for what was
And what is yet to come.
Watching the horseman
Pass by.

SHAKING REALISM

That morning the shaken realist
Woke to a dream that broke down
The dark tunnels of a mind filled
With sensations of himself.
Then to himself he said:

Words are more
Than mere material
Sunrises more
Than clouds and color
And light more
Than darkness

Must I dream only
The dream I know
Or can I know a dream
I never dreamed and so
Not a dream at all?

REGRETFULLNESS

The time has come to write
The poetry of regret
Not out of sadness
But from the surprise
Of unrepeatable moments
Of all we have been

Not the poetry of one moment only
But of a lifetime of moments
To celebrate what might have been
To realize the unrealizable
Was always part of reality
Part of the whole from which
We think ourselves
So resolutely remote

COMING HOME ON SUNDAY MORNING

September's green prepared us
For the stricter discipline
Of fallen leaves and bare wood
Without the soft support
Of summer colors,

Now September's breeze hints
Of shivers in the welcoming coolness
And morning coffee on the deck.
Recurrence is in the air, and
Something far, far off

Beckons from the dead of winter.

SOUND AND FURY

Beware the silent sign
Beyond the symbol
Untouchable distance
Inside the sacred shell
Of memory

Windless clouds
Dance alone unseen
By mind or world
Soundless infinities
Timeless searching
For simplicity

Emptiness a sign
Lost without a symbol
Fear is gone
And with it
Fearlessness

CAPPUCINNI CONVENTO AMALFI

We broke their statues
Drove them from their temples
But the gods are not dead.
C.P. Cavafy, *Ionic*

Here I first began to feel the force

Of old forms floating in the blue

Music of Mediterranean voices

Rising through smokey dust

Still lingering in lost sounds

Of monks breaking rocks and singing

Hoping to quell the savage ghosts

Still emerging from the long dead gods

Not yet buried by the pirates of the soul

BEFORE THE FALL
(*Thoughts on Round Bales and School Buses*)

Two pieces of nostalgia, pointing in different directions. Round bales are a reminder of how parts of the past can simply disappear: stacking a flatbed hay wagon with the old square bales is an art no longer practiced. What might have been a repeated rural scene of my loading a hay wagon from an old photograph simply no longer seems to exist in Floyd County (except perhaps as a staged reenactment). Parts of this past become holes in present reality.

School buses, by contrast, seem surprisingly resilient. The yellow buses that stop along the back roads of Floyd County early in the morning, as the children walk to get into them, are like a movie of my going to junior high school in 1958.

Since the past seemed covered by the mysteries of human memory, I searched for the true source of nostalgia in the natural world and found this poem as I drove along the Blue Ridge Parkway just before the full colors of fall were emerging.

Early Fall
(Before the Fall)

The trees speak the old nostalgias
The ones we cannot look for

The ones we cannot lose, unless
We choose to look for them, seeking

To find lost dreams of spring
In falling leaves of autumn

Or find the last light of spring
In the first colors of fall

FRAGMENT OUTSIDE TIME

In a penumbra of possibilities
Memory blinks while the sun
Slinks out of sight
Offering no excuses
For the darkness

REVISITATION

I have not yet returned
To the uneasiness of memory
Of the world without being
Or the inconstant meditation
Of a morning without evening
In the wild darkness of daylight.

Logic has been lost
In a forest of inequalities.

Time to return to the root
And find the day again
Buried in a tangle
Of words and meanings.

COLOSSUS REGAINED

Something vaguely feral
Sloughing into the sixties
Fatal to all forms
Of feigned indifference
My night shift was: reading
And now: remembrance
Scattered somewhere
In suburban silence
Louder than jackhammers
And more deadly.

AGAINST THE GRAIN

Along the ridge in early winter
Nature denies its own forces
Standing starkly in cold sunshine
The trees are done with their leaves
Done with the cycle of death and birth
Done with the green pain of spring
They will stand as they are now
Living forever in the silent light
Of the blue winter sky

FORM AS FORMLESSNESS

I was walking down 14th Street, reflecting on the Democritus and Atomism and the relationship between ancient atomism and modern and, in the process, wondering what connected the past with the present and future (one of the earliest philosophy papers I remember was one by someone with the last name "Will" with the title "Will the Future be Like the Past"). Philosophers of science are (or at least were) fond of understanding the concept of time by analyzing the role of the variable for time t in Newton's equations.

As I crossed 14th Street along L Street, my musing was interrupted by a passing bicycle. One of those red rental bicycles now common in Washington DC. I immediately – as it were in a flash – saw this bicycle as my answer to the question "What is the past?" – something we pick up at one point where we need it and drop off once we get to our destination, something that goes nowhere unless we peddle it, something we might not always want to own, something we paint red so we don't lose track of it, something that appears one way to us when we pick it up and another when we drop it off, and a million other connections yet to be made. I have no idea how to make sense of these reactions as philosophy, but I know they are the kernel of a poem – even though I have only a vague idea what the poem would look like.

Here is the difference between the poet and the philosopher: the philosopher would not see the bicycle; the poet would see only the bicycle. The philosopher, if he did see the bicycle, would proceed to explain it, the poet would find words to make it his or her own.

At that moment I knew I was neither a philosopher nor a poet. Although my instinct was to find words to make it my own, I found only these few lines from a vast poetic form I could no longer see.

This is the last of four stanzas. The first three were lost in a memory explosion and all attempts at recovery have failed.

The past is a red bicycle
Rented and reinvented
Returned as the latest
Name of God.

THIRTY WEST WYNEVA

This was the moment when reality came into view. Carol and I had an apartment at 30 West Wyneva Street in Philadelphia. It was around 3 am: I was asleep in our bed and Carol was awake next to me, reading. She woke me, excited from reading Ezra Pound's poem "An Object" because the lines, "This thing, which hath a code but not a core, hath set acquaintance where might have been affection, and nothing now disturbeth his reflection," struck her like an illumination.

Carol was the original existentialist. It was from her that I came to see the inevitability of thought in reality and reality in thought that will keep me wedded to philosophy for as long as I am alive – and later as long as my shade has some form of Dantean existence. What I remember to this day is the excitement in her voice at the new thought she found in the poem, a thought as palpable and hard as any objective fact. Nothing has ever brought that reality into view more clearly than that moment.

Snippets of Carol's phrases keep coming back to me. One I remember was: "Joy in a paint can and song in this wench." She would write these things on cocktail napkins at restaurants and then throw them out. This one came back to me when I was looking at an Instagram video of my daughter Marie and her friend Cameron stripping paint and I remembered repainting Carol's apartment when I was their age.

My favorite line of hers is one that came at the end of a series of verses she wrote as reflections on the nature of various animals. Each one was written on a three-by-five card and began with a phrase like, "When I consider the curious ways of a dog...." That was then followed by a commonsense explanation like, "I see they bark when they are afraid." (This is a poor imitation of what she wrote since she threw them out and I have lost any memory of these except the last one.) After reading several of these verses, you had the impression that behavior is explainable, and all is well. But the last one shifted the tone and said:

"When I consider the curious ways of man, I confess, my friend, I am puzzled."

As a philosopher and occasionally a poet, I am afraid that, forty-six years after Carol's death, these words are the most I can say about the behavior of human beings. As a paraphrase of Dostoyevsky, which Carol might have appreciated, I think of these as lost notes from Carol's underground.

OUR 20th CENTURY
(After Akhmatova)

I am my father's child

We are the 20th century

We are still forming

Still making poems

Timeless in a world

Without time

MOONSIGHT

I will leave on a beam of light.

Unbent but fallen

From the Cathedral of time.

Turning back

Before the dreamless night.

AfterImages

Retentions and Reflections

WORDS FOR PAINTING PERHAPS

As I sit here in the back room of the house, the snow across the back yard, under the apple tree and into the orchard, it feels like one of Whistler's London Nocturnes, with the dark wood against the backdrop of the snow and grey air awaiting the rising of sunlight over the mountaintop. Memories drift, painting a poem from long ago……..

The Apple Tree

This tree was here sixty years ago
When I thought I could live forever
Sitting beside the flowing creek
That became the lake that made
The scattered patterns
Of my life

DUST DOWN A COUNTRY ROAD

The allure of the light in the trees
  As late summer's green
  Starts to make its way
  Into softer shades of autumn.

Recalling a dream of light
  Passing this way
  Before human memory
  Before human song
  Gave voice to a land
  Now lost in roadside dust.

AS I LEAVE THE ROOM

I wonder have I lived

A phantom poet's life
In a world of philosophy

Or a phantom philosopher's
In a world of mathematics

A ghost in the world
The world thought
I was in.

A soul seeing light
In the shadow

REDEMPTION

I stripped away the shadows
Behind the barricades of darkness
Until I came
Face to face
With the Absolute
And found a face
Without absolution

ANACHRON

Always able to find the fault lines
Near the ridges of the mountain
Against the background of the past
Crossing the waters of lost poets

He never again found a new life
Reliving an old one, in a time
Of memories once vivid
Now lost without a past

SILKEN WEAVINGS

Poems are words
Woven into the weave of life
Silken threads of light
Along the edge
Of darkness

Unlocking
The cracks in the present
Keys to a place beyond time

Cadences connecting
A place not seen
To a sound not heard

LOST LANGUAGES

The voice of bright orange fire
Against the stark silence
Of a pure blue sky
Drives home
Joy
In
A
Sense
Of sacrifice
In dwindling light
Of approaching winter

FINDING THE FALCONER

Poetry resides within itself
Words outside the world
Turning and turning
Widening the world

Finding a place for another world
Not yet seen
Not yet heard
Beyond the reach
Of any word within

TIME AND AGAIN

There was music in the light
And dance in the darkness
Movements from before
Some ancient thoughts
Banished today's footsteps
From tomorrow's rivers

Until we made our peace
With those flowing streams
That tried to take away our dead
Branches and broken dreams
Before we could retrieve them
And make them live again.

CHRISTMAS BELOW ZERO

Let the trees paint the picture
Of chill in the wind at sunrise
Patterns on the wall
Moving soundlessly
Bending but not breaking
At daylight in this season
Of suffering and renewal.

Magic Horses

Early and Uncollected Poems

MAGIC HORSES

Magic horses come and go

Leaving tracks in fallen snow.

I had a vision of all times

People, places, jumbled rhymes.

PHAETON

Through night's quintessence,

Your reality fulgurates

Unearthed.............

.............unearthly.

I BUILT A CASTLE ONCE

I built a castle once

    Of passion, fire and waterfalls'

    Cascades of crimson love

    In mountain stream transparency

    I lived there with my lover.

Lost in time

    My castle falls

    Her clear streams freezing

    Her fiery hearth turns cold.

Without an architect of love

    I come to you

    Without construction or design

    Ethereal form

    In a life unbounded

    And unbinding.

DAY DAWNING

What day dawns, today,

That has not been before?

In earth's precession sun

And stars are moved and we

Know not the order of our

Being's chartless path

Between moments of our breath

Our spirit breathes

And we are free.

EAGLES FLY

Eagles fly, thunder, lightning

Shrink from fear's frozen frightening

Curse of Lethe harkening

Awareness to oblivion.

Horrors of a soul surceasing

Searing with a thought's elision

The spirit's subtle innocence.

GO OUTSIDE

Go outside, go outside

Away from here

Away from grey men waiting for cold food

With cold plates warmed by the sterile fire

Of sterno on silver settings.

Go outside, go outside

Where even the green worms

Fleeing the dust of earth

Climbing the yellow grass

Look for the blue air of day.

THE SHADE

I came to a well

Where a shade said to me

"Follow me down

and I'll set you free."

A dime in a meter

Brought me this hour

Now the sign reads,

"Violation, Expired"

We wander the shoreline

The shade and me,

But not on the beach

And not in the sea.

I reach in my pocket

For one more dime

Find only a hole

And a watch

With no time.

I swing at the shade

He holds fast my chains

Within myself

Nothing remains.

ICY NIGHT OF SIRIUS

Pilot did I choose this stream

That brought me to this land

Of pilgrims marching, single file?

Their cadenced step's a wintry rhyme

Freezing sights and sounds and words

In a gray monotone of solitude.

No more this deathless suffering!

Pilot let me see

In this icy night of Sirius

A gentle morn of spring.

FOOLISH HEART

Between the pleasure of advance

And the pain of retreat

Lies a world we seldom see

And never touch. In this impalpable

Region of the possible even clowns

Trick each other. Their performance

Knows no script, no words we comprehend

They neither laugh nor cry

But laugh and cry together

Their faces garish

In the stillness of frozen emotion.

The world between the pleasure

Of advance and the pain

Of retreat knows no time

No regrets and no

Salvation.

LOVE'S A HUMAN THING

Love's a human thing

No god could wish to see

It's torture and it torment

It's joy, it's ecstasy.

Love's a human thing

In gentleness it thrives

Without a smile it languishes

With a frown, it dies.

Love never is forever

It wasn't meant to stay

But it's written in eternity

If it only lasts a day.

CYCLES

The world is such a wondrous place

Though horror beauty can deface

Nothing ever is erased:

All returns itself to see

Nothing can alone be free

Nor anything alone esteemed

For the dreamer is the dream.

DECEMBER SUMMER

Fog fingers the edges of the bay

Lingering like words without declension

In cautious anticipation

Of this December-summer day.

Nature, too, confused by this unnatural season

Sprouts green grass under brown leaves

Uncertain of living and dying

Of beginnings and endings.

All the world is unfamiliar

Bathed in a warm hue out of time

A mist arresting the senses

Softness softly unsettling.

Master of the seasons,

Do you come to lift my spirits

Or dampen them? Better the bitter-cold

Death-ridden ravages of winter

Than this cruel and short reminder

Of a summer life now lost.

DEAD TREE IN FALL

You stand

Stark above the autumn greens

Of your neighbors

Bare as a naked old man

In a crowd.

Your ashen grey

Will not recede in spring

Your sap

Will not return.

You profit from the vision of the dead

Beyond the confusion of the leaves

Thoughts in tentacled branches

Penetrate the unknown.

DESERT SILENCE

Desert silence paints

Subtle sounds with colors

From the palate of the sun.

Time alone frames

The unoiled canvas

Of life and death.

TO RESTORE IS TO DESTROY

From the anthropologist's report
on Aberyswytch castle
(portions indecipherable.)

Stone fragments............

........channel winds........

............grass grows in....

..the kitchens................

EVENING IN NEW JERSEY

the monochrome of day

gives way

to the subtle pastels of dusk

gray, rose and slate-blue

colors of our common world

and uncommon love

two years have I lived

in your life

and you in mine

tonight the world

is large enough to love in

small enough to touch

touch in every way

NOTES ON POEMS

Venetian Lagoon is a variation on a line from Cassiodorus.

Milford Spring follows the rhyme and stanzaic structure of the *Ballad of Peach Tree Spring* by Wang Wei, from Vikram Seth's translation in *Three Chinese Poets*.

Above Ceasar's Head. Written by Howard Meroney, Highlands, North Carolina, 1932.

The Place of Solitude Where Three Dreams Cross. Title taken from T.S. Eliot, *Ash Wednesday, VI.*

Scholars at Dinner is a title given to a work by Athenaeus, a source for several of Sappho's lyrics.

Anachron is the name of an ancient author whose details I have forgotten.

Lost Languages arose as a reversal of Wittgenstein's idea that "To imagine a language is to imagine a form of life", imagining instead that the forms of the life of trees and the life of light are languages we have lost.

In *Time and Again* the ancient thoughts that banished footsteps are one way of looking at the famous line attributed to Heraclitus, typically translated as something like: 'You can't step into the same river twice'. But all translations of the remaining fragments are from later authors and largely speculation. One closer to the sense in play here is: 'The river where you set your foot just now is gone …' (fragment 41 as translated by Brooks Haxton)

Respects and apologies to artists whose words or thoughts I have appropriated or adapted:

> To William Butler Yeats for *Words for Painting Perhaps*
>   and *Finding the Falconer*
> To Wallace Stevens for *Silken Weavings* and *As I Leave the*
>   *Room*
> To John Hiatt for *Dust Down a Country Road*
> To Jackson Browne for *Redemption*

BIBLIOGRAPHY
(Sources for Quotations, In Order of Appearance)

Stevens, Wallace, et al. *The Collected Poems of Wallace Stevens*, Vintage Books, 1982, p. 342. In "Estetique du Mal", Wallace Stevens sees the world:

"As if the air, the mid-day air, was swarming
With the metaphysical changes that occur
Merely in living as and where we live."

Plato. *Loeb Classical Library: Plato III*, translated by W.R.M. Harvard University Press, p. 158.

"Poetry is Love's own craft, whereby all forms of life
Are begotten and produced."
Plato
The Symposium

Wittgenstein, Ludwig. *Tractatus Logico-Philosophicus*, translated by D.F. Pears & B.F. McGuinness. Routledge & Kegan Paul, 1961, p. 114.

"Die Grenzen der Sprache...
Die Grenzen meiner Welt bedueten."
Ludwig Wittgenstein
Tractatus Logico-Philosophicus

Bonnefoy, Yves. *Yves Bonnefoy Poems 1959-1975*, translated by Richard Pevear. Vintage Books, 1985, p. 48.

"Le silence
Est monte de ton livre vers ton coeur."
Un feu va devant nous

de Nerval, Gerard. *Gerard de Nerval Selected Writings,* translated by Richard Seiburth. Penguin Books, 1999, p. 374.

"..... de tous tes conseils l'univers est absent."
Gerard de Nerval
Vers Dores

Neruda, Pablo, et al. *The Book of Questions,* translated by William O'Daly. Copper Canyon Press, 1991.

"Qué hace una mosca encarcelada
en un soneto de Petrarca?"
Pablo Neruda
The Book of Questions

Wittgenstein, Ludwig. *Philosophical Investigations,* translated by G.E.M. Anscombe. Basil Blackwell & Mott, 1958, p. 8e.

"To imagine a language.....
...... is to imagine a form of life"
Ludwig Wittgenstein
Philosophical Investigations

Eliot, T.S. Four Quartets. Harcourt, Inc., 1971, p. 16.

"Only through time is time conquered."
T.S. Eliot
Four Quartets

Machado, Antonio. *Times Alone Selected Poems of Antonio Machado.* Wesleyan University Press, 1983, p. 131.

"The harp of Pythagoras goes on resonating in the silence.
Antonio Machado

Lu Yu. *The Wild Old Man Poems of Lu Yu*, translated by David M. Gordon. North Point Press, 1984, p. xi.

"Poetry comes ..... when no longer thinking about it."
Lu Yu

Southern, Richard William. *The Making of the Middle Ages*. Yale University Press, 1953, p. 87.

"It was in the face of the miraculous
that they became most human."
R.W. Southern
The Making of the Middle Ages

Stevens, Wallace, et al. "Sunday Morning," *The Collected Poems of Wallace Stevens*. Vintage Books, 1982, p. 71.

"Divinity must live within herself."
Wallace Stevens
Sunday Morning

Empedokles. *The Presocratic Philosophers*, translated by G.S. Kirk, J.E. Raven, and M. Schofield. Cambridge University Press, 1999, p. 316.

"In darkness they roam over the meadow."
Empedokles

Wittgenstein, Ludwig, et al. *Ludwig Wittgenstein Philosophical Remarks*, Raymond Hargreaves and Roger White. University of Chicago Press, 1975, p. 13.

"Memory and reality must be in one space."
Ludwig Wittgenstein

Cavafy, Constantine. *Complete Poems of Cavafy*, translated by Rae
    Delvin. Harcourt Brace, 1976, p. 32.

"We broke their statues
Drove them from their temples
But the gods are not dead."
                    C.P. Cavafy,
                    Ionic